A Million Dollars Worth of Tax

Table of Contents

Chapter 1 - American Dream Tax: Create, Duplicate and Execute	7
Chapter 2 - Profession in Taxation, What's It All About	14
Chapter 3 - What is a Business Partnership	20
Chapter 4 - The Virtual Assistant Platform	28
Chapter 5 - How to Become an Expert at Your Craft	34
Chapter 6 - Know Your Products Worth	39
Chapter 7 – Knowing Your Software	46
Chapter 8 - Customer Acquisition: What Beginners Need to Know	52
Chapter 9 - Customer Retention	57
Chapter 10 - Referral Marketing	62
Chapter 11 – Offering Other Services	71

Acknowledgement

To my beloved mother, Cansaday Fleming,

Your unwavering love, strength, and wisdom continue to guide me every day. Though you are no longer with us, your spirit lives on in every word of this book. This work is a tribute to your memory and the countless ways you have shaped my life.

Forever in my heart,
Brian

Chapter 1
American Dream Tax: Create, Duplicate, Execute

What is duplication?

The practice of doing the same thing more than once or having more than one person or thing to do the same task, when this is not necessary.

Growth by Duplication

Growth by duplication is taking your present business and duplicating it in other locations. It's also called a "cookie-cutter" approach because as with a cookie cutter, identical cookies can efficiently be stamped out in either small or large numbers.

There is a margin of safety in pursuing this method of growth because your expansion does not take you outside your already proven circle of competence. You are sticking to what you know best and what you have already proven to be successful. This approach does, however, require some management skills beyond those required for operating a single location.

Small- and Large-Scale Duplication

With small scale duplication assume you have a profitable business that is appropriate for duplication and your customers are located in a ten-mile radius. If you add another equally successful store outside that area (so you're not competing with yourself) you could accomplish two goals:

- Double your sales.
- Potentially more than double your earnings since some fixed costs are now spread over two stores and you have greater purchasing power.

With large scale duplication if you build a really large business, you will continue to expand over an increasingly widespread area. Your long-term goals could include:

- Franchising the concept.
- Public ownership.
- Become a candidate for acquisition by a larger company.

Management Skill Needed

Duplication requires successful management in a number of business disciplines unrelated to the operation of the stores themselves. Failure in any one of them could become a stumbling block.

- **Financing skills**: Opening a new store location will cost a lot of money. Assuming you are leasing the location, costs will include fixtures, equipment, tenant improvements, inventory, signage, lease deposits, working capital and other expenses. Your sources of funding will come from retained earnings or borrowing or both.
- **Create profit centers**: Incentive plans will vary according to the business, but one essential component will be a system based on frequently calculated profit and loss statements for each individual store.
- **Management selection**: The success of your growth will depend a great deal on how skilled you and your human resources (HR) management is in selecting the best managers to run your stores. Mistakes made in this process can result in a huge drain on earnings.
- **Accounting oversight**: Your accounting system will require a system of preparing frequent income statements on a store-by-store basis. Profit sharing payments should be disbursed to managers at the same time as the profit and loss (P & L) statements are prepared. This will require your accounting department to develop procedures to accomplish this including inventory accounting.

- **Supervision oversight**: Once you have opened your second store you are now a chain and will require some controls in place.

10 DO's

1. Stay in the business that is within your circle of competence.
2. Stay within geographical limits you can service well.
3. Prove profitability and systems before expanding.
4. Bring in your lawyer for all real estate transactions.
5. Build out one market area at a time.
6. Verify that your name, logos, and slogans are available.
7. Compartmentalize your P & L's to individual stores.
8. Calculate P & L's frequently for each store.
9. Establish a real estate site model.
10. Pay fair rent for a great location.

10 DONT's

1. Over borrow. Maintain 3-5 times cash flow-to-debt service.
2. Pay great rent for a fair location.
3. Risk duplication if you are the sole key person.
4. Be in a hurry… instead, proceed with great caution.
5. Overlook the importance of operating manuals.
6. Let leasing agents negotiate your leases.
7. Overlook the importance of demographics.
8. Be vulnerable to Website-based competition.
9. Give stock to managers: share the profits instead.
10. Sign a lease without including recommended deal points.

A MILLION DOLLARS WORTH OF TAX

A MILLION DOLLARS WORTH OF TAX

Chapter 2
Profession in Taxation, What's It All About

The tax profession is full of the most charming, eloquent, intelligent and modest people you could wish to meet. Benjamin Franklin is quoted saying:
"Our new Constitution is now established, everything seems to promise it will be durable; but, in this world, nothing is certain except death and taxes."

What Is It About Taxes?

The tax industry is an incredibly stable profession, regardless of boom or bust, depression, recession or growth. People often joke about death and taxes being the only thing you can count on in life! After all, regardless of the economic climate, the government still collects taxes. The UK has the most complex tax system in the world.

How Many People in the U.S. File Taxes

The IRS reported that as of December 2022, approximately 152,089,000 tax returns were e-filed for tax year 2021 out of a total of 165,774,000 of 2021 tax returns filed.

Taxes and the U.S.

Tax is collected from every person or organization which receives or buys something of value. For example: salary, business revenue, fuel, inheritance, home, etc.

The Benefits of a Job in Tax

- Fast Changing Industry
  - Tax law is updated every year with the Finance Bill, combined with European and international law changes means that working in taxes offers a highly stable, secure and high paying career option.
- Tax is Jurisdictional
  - This means that U.S. tax is only relevant to U.S. taxpayers which means there will be jobs in the U.S.
- Everyone is Subject to Taxes
  - Individuals and businesses all require advice and support from tax professionals to comply with tax laws.
- Culturally Diverse Population
  - Increasingly more culturally diverse populations of tax professionals are entering the field and climbing their own ladder of success.

Will I Like Working in Tax?

- Well, are you:
    - Detail oriented.
    - Creative and strategic.
    - Good with numbers.
    - A Team Builder.

What Qualifications Do Good Tax Professionals Have?

- Problem Solving: Entrepreneurial, lateral thinking, problem solving.
- Empathetic: You are dealing with other people's taxes and finances, so you need to understand them and their issues.
- Literate: Able to write reasonably well
- Communication Skills: Ability to convey complex information in a simple manner suitable for the client.

What Would I actually do?

A tax trainee typically starts out with training to show you how to do basic duties such as entering client information into a tax preparation software program. Then, under supervision, progress on to following:

- Preparation of tax accounting calculations
- Analysis of data

- Carry out tax research and summarize findings.
- Meet clients as part of the tax team.
- Learning about corporation tax and helping businesses comply.
- Learn about PAYE and draft PAYE advice.
- Responding to HMRC correspondence and assisting with enquiries.
- Preparation of tax notes for accounts and reporting.
- Respond to queries from finance functions and auditors.

A MILLION DOLLARS WORTH OF TAX

A MILLION DOLLARS WORTH OF TAX

Chapter 3
What is a Business Partnership

A business partnership is a legal agreement between two or more entities that determines shared ownership and operation of a business. A partnership may be between two people, two businesses, or shared among any number of people and organizations.

Why Have Partners?

Partnership could mean your business will have access to new products, reach a new market, block a competitor (through an exclusive contract) or increase customer loyalty. Some prefer to use partnerships to strengthen weak aspects of their business. Here are a few more reasons:

1. Important connections and resources as we conduct our jobs, plan for the future, and build our knowledge about products, changes and trends.
2. Business partner relationships can help us when a product or service changes or when an additional product or service is needed.

Advantages of Partnership

1. You have an extra set of hands.

    a. When you have a business partner, you have a person—or multiple people—who can help you with all the business tasks. The partners can divide up tasks, meaning tasks will get done faster and the partners might be able to tackle more than if they worked alone.
2. You have less financial burden.
    a. A partner can ease your financial burden. Instead of paying for everything yourself, your partner can split the cost. Because of the partner's financial contributions, you might be able to avoid large amounts of debt when starting your business.
3. You benefit from additional knowledge.
    a. Partners can bring skills and knowledge to your business that you don't have. You might have a lot of knowledge about the product or service your business provides, but not know how to run a business. You can bring on a partner who is skilled at running a business.
4. There is less paperwork.
    a. All partners involved must sign a partnership agreement. This agreement will detail the duties and responsibilities of each partner, how decisions will be made, how profits and

losses are divided, and more. Creating and signing this document is simpler than filling out the paperwork for other business structures.

Disadvantages of Partnerships

1. You can't make decisions on your own.
    a. You cannot act independently when you're in a partnership. You must work with your partner to make decisions. If your partner does act alone and makes a reckless decision, all partners are responsible for the decision and results. A reckless partner cannot be held solely responsible.
2. You have to spit profits.
    a. When you run a business by yourself, you have an opportunity to gain all the profits from the business. But when you have a partnership, you have to share the profits. Depending on how many partners you have, your share of the profits can get fairly small.
3. You aren't separate from the business.
    a. A partnership is not a separate legal entity from you and the other partners. All partners are legally and financially responsible for the business. If your business faces legal

problems, you won't be considered separately from your business. And, if your business isn't able to pay back debts, debt collectors can come after your personal money.
4. You will have disagreements.
    a. Anytime you get people together at work, there's potential for conflict. You and your partners will have disagreements. You might even get sick of working with each other. If this happens, you can't easily dissolve the partnership. Hopefully, you've drawn up a partnership exit strategy.

The Importance of Partnerships

The partnership is crucial to the growth of any business venture. Merchants and traders from time immemorial have made use of the principle of a strategic partnership to conduct their businesses; the trend is still very much applicable today. A partnership manifests itself in different forms, ranging from business owners cooperating to investing in a project to share technical knowledge and ideas between firms. Whatever any business does, it is important to look for the right partnership agreement that benefits both parties.

How to Find a Business Partner

A business partner is someone with whom you legally share the co-ownership of your company, including any profits or losses. This relationship should be carefully outlined to ensure both parties understand their financial and professional obligations, as you may share your financial resources in addition to skills and expertise.

1. Evaluate your colleagues.
    a. Your former and current colleagues could make ideal candidates for a business partnership. Because you have a work history, you already know what this person is like in a professional environment.
2. Collaborate with friends.
    a. Friends can make excellent business partners when your skills, education and experience complement each other. Rather than selecting a close friend with the same expertise as you, look for friends or acquaintances that excel in areas you're less familiar with.
3. Attend industry events.
    a. Industry events—conferences, lectures and trade shows—can present great opportunities for a potential business partnership because

           they bring together people with the same interests.
4. Explore online entrepreneur networks.
    a. Several websites and online networks exist for people seeking business partners.
    b. These virtual communities typically allow you to create your own profile and browse others.

A MILLION DOLLARS WORTH OF TAX

A MILLION DOLLARS WORTH OF TAX

Chapter 4

The Virtual Assistant Platform

A virtual assistant is an independent contractor who provides administrative services to clients while operating outside of the client's office. A virtual assistant typically operates from a home office but can access the necessary planning documents, such as shared calendars, remotely.

How a Virtual Assistant Works

Virtual assistants have become more prominent as small businesses and startups rely on virtual offices to keep costs down and businesses of all sizes increase their use of the internet for daily operations. Because a virtual assistant is an independent contractor, a business does not have to provide the same benefits or pay the same taxes that it would for a full-time employee.

Virtual Assistant Qualifications

A virtual assistant should be tech-savvy, having a wide range of computer skills and a high level of proficiency with commonly used software and business programs. A virtual assistant who specializes in bookkeeping should be adept at basic accounting tasks, such as account reconciliations and double-entry bookkeeping.

Benefits of a Virtual Assistant

For small business owners, hiring a virtual assistant can help them free up valuable hours to focus on growing the business and generating revenue. It can be easier and more cost-effective to outsource tasks that are tedious and time-consuming, to someone who is skilled at them.

How to Hire a Virtual Assistant

With the increasing number of freelance contractors who work from home, the employment market has seen a proliferation of Web-based companies that serve as intermediaries between prospective employers and contractors. Some freelancer sites have enormous work pools made up of individuals across the globe with a wide range of experience and expertise. On these sites, clients can post details about the type of tasks they need the virtual assistant to perform and the maximum rate they are willing to pay. Freelance workers may then bid on the job and give the client samples of their work for review. In some cases, the client can set up a video conference to interview the applicants and to assess their qualifications more thoroughly.

4 Reasons Why You Need a Virtual Assistant

1. Lower training costs.

2. Boost efficiency by outsourcing non-care tasks.
3. Frees up time for strategic thinking.
4. Reduced micromanagement.

Lower Training Costs

You can also save on training costs by hiring virtual professionals. Think about it. When you hire a first-time employee, you'll have to invest considerable time and resources into training them for different aspects of their job. However, VAs only work on specific tasks they excel at, so you won't have to worry about strenuous onboarding. They can get started right away!

Boost efficiency by Outsourcing Non-core Tasks

Companies and entrepreneurs deal with many non-core activities like. Sending emails and newsletters, Handling customer queries, Internet research, Scheduling meetings, Data entry etc. While these are necessary tasks, they're not core tasks that need to be done by an in-house team. Asking your in-house employees to do these small tasks takes away time they could spend on things that need to be done in person.

Frees Up Time for Strategic Thinking

Virtual assistants can perform your non core tasks, giving you more time to focus on growing your business. Rather than wasting time and resources on day-to-day operations, business owners can focus on strategic leadership for long-term growth. This helps you to set goals that guide your company for better performance and long-term success.

Reduced Micromanagement

Because virtual assistants offer a specialized skill set, you'll only have to provide the job description once. Also, since they are used to handling multiple clients and tasks at a time, they're usually good at time management and ensuring timely deliveries. That's why you wouldn't need to worry about checking on virtual assistants constantly, allowing you to focus on core business activities. Meanwhile, your assistant can carry out their duties with consistency and ease.

A MILLION DOLLARS WORTH OF TAX

A MILLION DOLLARS WORTH OF TAX

Chapter 5

How to Become an Expert at Your Craft

Becoming an expert in your field can fast-track your status and increase your earning potential in your industry. Your expertise has the potential to make you more desirable as a job candidate or more valuable within your current company. Learning the steps you can take to become an expert in a particular subject can help you evaluate if you're ready to master a specific skill.

How Long Does It Take to Become an Expert?

There is no definitive answer for the amount of time it takes to become an expert. While some suggest that devoting 10,000 hours to studying and practicing a subject or skill helps you achieve the level of expert, others believe that for some people it could take 20,000 to 25,000 hours to truly master a subject. Additionally, not all skills are the same and some skills may require far less than 10,000 hours to master, while others may require far more.

Can Anyone Become an Expert?

Whether you can become a master in a particular subject, skill or activity is only something you can determine after you try. Deliberate practice is where you practice things outside of your comfort zone and move beyond your current skill level which is necessary for improving your skills. However, there is no way to definitively say whether anyone can become an expert with the right amount of practice and training. Depending on the subject or skill, genuine, inherent talent may be needed to be an expert, but for others, sheer motivation and concerted, consistent effort might make the difference between an amateur and an expert.

How to Become an Expert

1. Identify what you're interested in.
2. Focus on one task at a time.
3. Start with what is most important.
4. Invest time and effort.
5. Set specific goals.
6. Engage in deliberate practice.
7. Find or create an environment for practice.
8. Look for specific and accurate feedback.
9. Find a mentor.
10. Focus on progression.

Benefits of Becoming an Expert

1. Experts are more likely to be listened to and regarded well for their skill.
2. People trust experts and are more likely to believe your opinion when you know more.

3. Experts have a greater likelihood to make more money in their career.
4. Instead of working to create a peer network, they are drawn into one.

Never become so much of an expert that you stop gaining expertise. View life as a continuous learning experience.

A MILLION DOLLARS WORTH OF TAX

A MILLION DOLLARS WORTH OF TAX

Chapter 6
Know Your Products Worth

A fee is a payment to a professional person or to a professional or public body in exchange for advice or services. There are different types of fees:

- **A La Carte Fees**
    - Fees can also be charged in situations in which a customer requests additional services.
- **Service Fees**
    - A fee collected to pay for services that relate to a product or service that is being purchased.
- **Fee-For-Service**
    - A payment model where services are unbundled ad paid for separately.

How Fees Work

Fees are most often associated with transactional relationships, specifically to professionals who provide services. In some cases, a fee is charged when an individual hires a business to do a specific task, such as cleaning a house or filing taxes. This type of fee is often the most transparent and transactional, as it represents payment for the sole reason a fee-charging business was hired.

How Much Should I Charge for My Product?

Figuring out how much to charge is a challenging part of doing business. Whether you are a freelancer or a small business owner, figuring out how much to charge for your products or services can be tricky. There is plenty of math involved, n addition to knowing your customers and anticipating their emotional response to your pricing. How much to charge depends on many factors:

- Cost-Plus Pricing: Price = [Cost + Expense] + Profit
- Demand Pricing: Profit = Price − [Cost + Expense]
- Competitive Pricing

Cost-Plus Pricing: Price = [Cost + Expense] + Profit

Sometimes known as markup pricing, this model builds a profit into your product pricing strategy. Cost-Plus Pricing is simply that: a price that covers your costs (e.g., the amount of money it takes to have the product for sale) plus some markup for profit. Using cost-plus pricing allows you to plan for financial success. However, there is a downside. If you've overestimated your sales for one month, and fewer items are sold, you may not be able to cover the costs of producing your product.

Demand Pricing: Profit = Price − [Cost + Expense]

Demand-Based Pricing takes into account the demand for a particular product, adjusting prices to fit how a customer perceives value. A common example of demand pricing Is the airline industry. A ticket price will change based on the holiday season or during spring break. This type of pricing works well with services as well. For instance, if a particular stylist is booked months in advance, the salon may raise the price per service. Demand pricing can be very sensitive, but if you notice that you can't keep up with demand for your product, you may be undercharging. Try raising prices incrementally and observing how sales numbers and profits are affected.

Competitive Pricing

Competitive pricing is the least complicated option as it involves seeing what other, similar retailers charge for their products. Keep in mind that if your product is of higher quality, the price should reflect that – and vice versa for a lower -quality product. Make sure that in addition to looking at market prices, you price to cover your costs and expenses. Many product verticals regularly provide manufacturer's suggested retail pricing (MSRP) to guide merchants on a pricing strategy. This is another great resource that you can use to calculate our unique pricing model.

Flat-Rate Billing

The benefit of flat-rate billing for clients is that they know the amount that they have to pay for the project beforehand so there is little room for dispute. (Author Unknown)

How to Charge for a Service

Freelancers and service-based businesses can use the above pricing models to price their services. While it is often less straightforward to calculate your service expenses, there are costs you will need to cover in addition to making a profit. A free lance designer may need to cover expenses such as an InDesign subscription, printing costs and a portion of their health insurance and self-employment taxes. These expenses will form the basis for what you charge, plus more depending on your time commitment or level of expertise. The fee to charge can be one of the following:

- Hourly Rate
- Flat Fee
- Variable Pricing

Hourly Rate

The service provider charges per hour, with a rate that is determined by your level of expertise or seniority. The SBA suggests including travel time as an extra charge. The main benefit of this model is that you are compensated for the amount of time and effort you spend on a particular project. This option works well for long-term projects rather than sort or irregular jobs.

Flat Fee

Flat rates work well for projects with definite deliverables and well-defined scope of work, or projects for which the time commitment required Is difficult to estimate. In this scenario, the service provider charges a set fee that can be paid up front or at regular intervals until the project is finished. According to FreshBooks an online accounting tool, "The benefit of flat-rate billing for the clients is that they know the amount they have to pay for the project beforehand so there is little room for dispute." (Freshbooks.com)

Variable Pricing

Finally, variable pricing is a model in which different customers are charged different rates. Bargaining and negotiation help set the price for each customer where you may wish to reward bigger contracts with a small hourly discount or create a loyalty pricing tier for your best customers. If you choose this option, make sure you are able to justify why different clients are charged different prices.

A MILLION DOLLARS WORTH OF TAX

A MILLION DOLLARS WORTH OF TAX

Chapter 7
Knowing Your Software

Software is in everything and it's everywhere. Software is behind the scenes of making every work from cars, houses and computers. Software not only makes your computer hardware perform important tasks but can also help your business work more efficiently. The right software can even lead to new ways of working. It is therefore a crucial business asset, and you should choose your software carefully so that it matches your business needs.

What is Software?

Software is a set of instructions, data or programs used to operate computers and execute specific tasks. It is the opposite of hardware, which describes the physical aspects of a computer. Software is a generic term used to refer to applications, scripts and programs that run on a device. It can be thought of as the variable part of a computer, while hardware is the invariable part.

What Are the Main Business Software Types?

Presentations: They are communication tools that can be used as demonstrations, lectures, speeches, reports, and more. It is mostly presented before an audience.

Accounting Software

Like it or not, accounting is an integral part of your business, whether you're a sole operator or hire hundreds of employees worldwide. Ensuring your company's financial records are accurate and updated will make monitoring your business's financial health that much easier while ensuring you remain tax compliant. Many great accounting software options range from basic to elite packages depending on your individual needs. Under the umbrella of accounting software, you can consider a number of innovative features.

Customer Relationship Management Software (CRM)

A valuable way to better analyze and assess your business's interaction with its customers and identify areas of improvement. It's important to note that not all customers are alike, and for companies to better target a specific audience, it's necessary to have an overview of data that allows for this. CRM software offers you access to real time data through effective reporting, making your company more competitive. This is because understanding what your client base actually wants allows you to better strategize your marketing campaigns and budget accordingly.

Sales, Marketing, and PR Software

At some point, you're going to look at reaching new audiences or letting existing customers know more about your products or new launches. For more impactful customer engagement, it's beneficial to have some understanding of the existing sales to determine what works and what doesn't. By implementing sales, marketing and PR software, you're better prepared to take on competitors through increased insight using real-time data. This also allows you to adapt a marketing strategy if it's not achieving its targets.

Inventory Management

Inventory management just makes sense. Keeping your digital finger on the pulse of your business means knowing what's coming in versus what's going out in order to keep your customers happy. The larger the business, the more you'll need a solid inventory management tool to stay on top of stock at various locations, reduce the risk of obsolete products, refill fastmoving goods, and keep on top of changing customer preferences.

7 Steps for Choosing the Right Business Software

1. Decide who needs to be involved in decision-making.
2. Review your processes, prioritize your needs and set your budget.
3. Do your research.
4. Get the right advice.

5. Select the software you want to emo or trial.
6. Train your team.
7. Communicate about new features and updates.

A MILLION DOLLARS WORTH OF TAX

A MILLION DOLLARS WORTH OF TAX

Chapter 8

Customer Acquisition: What Beginners Need to Know

What is Customer Acquisition?

Put simply, customer acquisition refers to gaining new consumers. Acquiring new customers involves persuading consumers to purchase a company's products and/or services. Companies and organizations consider the cost of customer acquisition as an important measure in evaluating how much value customers bring to their businesses.

Why is Customer Acquisition Important?

Customer acquisition is critical for creating a firm and developing a foothold in the market, from bringing in new clients to increasing revenue. It aids in the acquisition of new clients for your company. More clients mean more income, which means more profit for your company.

Benefits of Customer Acquisition

Good Attention: It motivates clients to check out your products and services. This not only boosts revenue but also attracts new clients to your company.

Consistent Revenue Guaranteed: This attracts potential customers to your company. Customers who are old and regular customers of your items are considered potential customers.

New Client Alert: It aids in the acquisition of new clients for your company. More clients mean more income, which means more profit for your company.

How to Measure Customer Acquisition

Conversion rate: It measures the percentage of people who completed a process after starting it. To make the most of this measurement, be sure to clarify what you mean by "start" and "end" of a process.

Customer Acquisition Cost (CAC)

Dividing marketing costs by the number of consumers obtained is a typical method for calculating customer acquisition costs.

The Rate of New Customer Acquisition

Compare client acquisition rates over different periods to see if your results are increasing over time. It's computed by multiplying the number of consumers acquired over a given period by the length of that period.

How to Improve Customer Acquisition

Your client acquisition plan isn't set in stone once you've created it. As your product, company, marketplace, rivals, buyers, and marketing trends change, it should evolve as well. You can do a few things to boost your customer acquisition outcomes.

- Because most first-time website visitors aren't going to buy your stuff, build consumer engagement. As consumers come to know your brand, engaging them will allow you to create trust.
- Rather than hiring a huge sales crew, automate as much of your marketing and lead the nurturing process as feasible.

Quick Tips to Keep in Mind

Referral programs: Customer referral programs allow your loyal customers to acquire new customers for you.

Brand communities: Brand communities act as an acquisition tool through the desire to be a part of something exclusive.

Strategic advertisement: Strategic advertising is more efficient and effective than traditional, aggressive advertising.

Value-add Marketing: Value-add marketing lets you acquire customers through quality content.

A MILLION DOLLARS WORTH OF TAX

A MILLION DOLLARS WORTH OF TAX

Chapter 9
Customer Retention

Customer retention is the rate at which customers will stay with a business for a given period of time. This happens if a positive relationship between the company and the customer already exists.

Why is Customer Retention So Important?

- It helps success.
  - For many businesses, customer retention/churn is a Key Performance Indicators (KPI) because a company's ability to retain existing customers is fundamental to both its short-term and long-term success.
- Word of Mouth.
  - Happy customers can often lead to gaining new customers through referrals.
- It's Cheaper.
  - It is often much cheaper to retain existing customers than acquire new ones. Sales and marketing acquisition costs usually greatly outweigh costs related to customer service and ongoing customer satisfaction.
- Loyalty.

- Loyal customers tend to be repeat customers, meaning they are valuable. Increasing customer retention increases the chance that a customer will become a loyal, repeat customer and can massively increase profits.

Why Customer Retention, Do I really Need It?

It is clear that customer retention should not only be an important metric, but a core goal of almost every business. Remember it is always more expensive to acquire a new customer than to retain an old one.

Benefits of Customer Retention

1. Retained customers tend to buy other services from the same company.
2. Retained customers are known to be less price/cost sensitive.
3. Positive work of mouth is free marketing 24/7.

How to Calculate Retention

Research your customers to find out what your customers need most. To calculate our customer retention rate (CRR) you can use the following simple formula involving the customers you have at the start (S), at the end (E), and customers acquired during the period you are measuring (N).

It looks like this: **CRR = ((E-N)/S) x 100**

The C's of Retention

Keep these in mind when thinking of your customers:

- Clarity
- Convenience
- Choice
- Communication
- Cost
- Control
- Consistency
- Connection

A MILLION DOLLARS WORTH OF TAX

A MILLION DOLLARS WORTH OF TAX

Chapter 10
Referral Marketing

A referral program is a word-of-mouth marketing tactic that encourages customers to advocate on behalf of your brand. Rather than writing reviews online, or submitting customer feedback surveys, referral programs let customers share their brand experience with partners, colleagues, and friends.

This approach not only lowers acquisition costs but also increases customer loyalty. To begin, establish clear objectives for your referral program, such as increasing the overall client base or boosting seasonal appointments. Consider what motivates your current clients and how those motivations can be aligned with your business goals to create a compelling offer.

The purpose of a referral program is to attract new leads to your business. But you're not just bringing in anyone. By asking customers to think about people who would benefit from your product or service, they'll refer leads that are a good fit for your brand.

- **Identify your target audience:** Understand who your current clients are and who they are likely to refer to. Tailor your referral program to fit their networks.

- **Set clear referral objectives:** Determine what you aim to achieve with your referral program, such as increasing specific service usage or client numbers during off-peak times.
- **Choose an enticing incentive:** Decide on rewards that encourage participation without undercutting your profit margin. Options might include discounts, service upgrades, or free additional consultations.
- **Communicate clearly:** Make sure your clients understand how the referral program works and what benefits they will gain from participating. Effective communication can be achieved through emails, flyers, or during face-to-face consultations.

Building a Referral Marketing Program

A successful referral marketing program requires a strategic approach that encompasses not only the creation of the program but also its promotion and monitoring. Start by designing marketing materials that explain the benefits of the program. Use testimonials and data to show potential referrers the tangible benefits that others have gained. Develop a tracking system to monitor referrals, ensuring that both referrers and referees receive their promised rewards promptly, which reinforces trust and encourages ongoing participation.

- **Develop marketing materials:** Create brochures, emails, and webpage content that explain the referral program clearly.
- **Leverage testimonials:** Use success stories from satisfied clients to illustrate the benefits of your services and the referral program.
- **Implement a tracking system:** Use software or databases to keep track of referrals and ensure accurate reward distribution.
- **Regularly review and adjust:** Monitor the effectiveness of your referral marketing program and adjust as needed to improve participation rates and client satisfaction.

Building a Referral Program That Converts

Conversion is key in referral programs; you want every mention of your service to potentially lead to a new client. The design of the program should make referring as easy as possible and rewarding enough to motivate clients to act. Focus on creating a seamless process for both referrers and new clients, minimizing barriers to participation such as complicated sign-up procedures or unclear program rules.

- **Simplify the referral process:** Ensure the referral process is straightforward—consider a simple online form or dedicated referral app. Make it easy for your customers to refer others.

- **Focus on high conversion rewards:** Offer rewards that are immediately appealing and relevant to your clients' interests and needs.
- **Educate your clients:** Regularly inform your clients about how the referral program works and remind them of the benefits they can gain.
- **Measure and optimize:** Use analytics to track the effectiveness of different aspects of the program and make data-driven decisions to enhance conversion rates.
- **Use Catchy Headlines:** Headlines are a key player in attracting your customers to join. It should provide the gist of the program in a single sentence and explain the benefits of joining. Here are a few examples of headlines that work:
    1. Give $20, Get $20.
    2. Refer a friend and get $15.
    3. Share a better way of working.
    4. Spread the word and receive a gas card.

Most referral software tools provide a variety of user-friendly sharing options such as social media, email, and text message. It's advisable to include a one-click referral link that customers can easily copy and paste for sharing in their preferred method.

Implementing a user-friendly referral widget that allows subscribers to share coupons via email, Facebook, Twitter, or directly through a link is an effective strategy. This widget also pre-fills the email with the referral message, streamlining the sharing process to just a few simple clicks.

In addition to sharing options, crafting effective referral messaging is crucial. This is the text your customer will share with their friend. Providing a pre-filled message ready to send can simplify the referral process, making it easier for customers to promote your business. Utilizing well-established referral program templates can often yield better results. The referral message is likely the first interaction they will have with your business, so your referral message template should:

- Start by clearly explaining the benefits of the referral.
- Include a clear call to action indicating the next steps.
- Ensure the message is straightforward and easy to comprehend.
- Personalize the message to enhance engagement.

Choosing Your Referral Program Rewards

The choice of rewards can significantly impact the success of a referral program. Select rewards that resonate with your clientele while ensuring they are economically viable for your business. Consider a mix of immediate perks for referrals and more substantial rewards for conversions to actual clients. This dual-benefit structure encourages more participation and higher conversion rates.

- **Evaluate reward options:** Assess different types of rewards such as cash, discounts, or complementary services to determine what best motivates your clients.
- **Balance appeal and cost:** Choose rewards that are attractive to your clients but also cost-effective for your business.
  - Store Credit or points.
  - Service upgrades or freebies.
  - Free products.
  - Company swag.
  - External gift cards.
  - Donations to charity.
  - Discounts coupons.

- **Offer tiered rewards:** Implement a tiered reward system that incentivizes multiple referrals, increasing customer engagement.
- **Get feedback:** Regularly solicit feedback from participants to find out what rewards they find most appealing and why.

By effectively implementing these strategies within your tax preparation business, you can build a robust referral marketing system that enhances both client acquisition and retention while driving sustainable growth.

A MILLION DOLLARS WORTH OF TAX

A MILLION DOLLARS WORTH OF TAX

Chapter 11
Offering Other Services

Expanding Through Conglomerate Strategies

A conglomerate is a corporation of several different, sometimes unrelated, businesses. In a conglomerate, one company owns a controlling stake in several smaller companies, conducting business separately and independently. Conglomerates often diversify business risk by participating in many different markets.

Understanding Conglomerates

Conglomerates are large parent companies made up of smaller independent entities that may operate across multiple industries. Each of a conglomerate's subsidiary businesses runs independently of the other business divisions, but the subsidiaries' managers' report to the senior management of the parent company. Many conglomerates are thus multinational and multi-industry corporations.

Benefits of Offering Other Services

Diversification of business enables the company to diversify its business. It helps to overcome risks associated with the vulnerable market. Utilization of excess cash when a business has excess cash but does not have enough opportunity to expand in its sector, then the business invests such excess cash into another company of a different sector to utilize the idle funds.

Disadvantages of Offering Other Services
- **Shift in Focus:** Management requires a lot of effort to understand the new business sector, operations of the business, etc.
- **Complication:** It leads to the merger of different human values and employees who have experience working in various industries. This leads to complications in human relationships and behavior.

Why You Should Offer Other Services

You can get more customers and more sales. This may sound pretty obvious, but it's funny how many small business owners overlook this idea. More services can likely equal more customers. That's because people have varied needs. If they don't find what they're looking for at your establishment, they may quickly go elsewhere.

Ways to Add New Services to Your Small Business
- Learn what the market needs:
  - If you're close to your customers, you may already know what services and products they need. But it helps to confirm your gut instinct. Send out customer surveys, conduct

informal interviews, and do online market research. You might learn something new.
- Consider areas where you already have training:
    - It's tricky to learn a completely new skill. Do you have skills up your sleeve that meet your customers' needs? If so, it'll feel natural to add a new service to your business. If you do need additional training to offer something new, consider the costs and benefits. It may be worth it.
- Revisit your business plan:
    - Did you make a small business plan at the get-go? It's time to revisit it. A solid business plan can help you identify your target market, their needs, and help you map out a plan to win over competitors.
- Get creative:
    - There are two ways to offer new services. The first is to create a completely new offering. The second is to create a new version of your current offering. Like ice cream, you can have one, main product with many different flavors. Decide which approach works best for your business. Then sit down to brainstorm. Get creative and

don't cut out any ideas until your brainstorming session is done.

A MILLION DOLLARS WORTH OF TAX

A MILLION DOLLARS WORTH OF TAX

A MILLION DOLLARS WORTH OF TAX

A MILLION DOLLARS WORTH OF TAX

A MILLION DOLLARS WORTH OF TAX

A MILLION DOLLARS WORTH OF TAX

A MILLION DOLLARS WORTH OF TAX

A MILLION DOLLARS WORTH OF TAX

A MILLION DOLLARS WORTH OF TAX

A MILLION DOLLARS WORTH OF TAX

A MILLION DOLLARS WORTH OF TAX

A MILLION DOLLARS WORTH OF TAX

A MILLION DOLLARS WORTH OF TAX

A MILLION DOLLARS WORTH OF TAX

www.ingramcontent.com/pod-product-compliance
Lightning Source LLC
Chambersburg PA
CBHW050335010526
44119CB00004B/154